HISTORY OF THE FORTRESS OF GWALIOR

HISTORY OF THE FORTRESS OF GWALIOR

By

SHRIMANT BALWANT ROW
BHAYASAHEB, SCINDIA

GYAN

Published by

GYAN

Gyan Publishing House
5, Ansari Road
Daryaganj, New Delhi-110002
Phone: 011-47034999, 9811692060
E-mail: books@gyanbooks.com

Distribution Network
gyanbooks.com
India, USA, Canada, UK, Australia, France

ISBN : 978-81-212-9830-8 (PB)
First Published, 1892

2nd Impression 2023

Printed at: Gyan Press, Delhi.

HISTORY OF THE FORTRESS OF GWALIOR
Author: SHRIMANT BALWANT ROW BHAYASAHEB, SCINDIA

HISTORY OF THE FORTRESS

OF

GWALIOR

BY

SHRIMANT BALWANT ROW BHAYASAHEB,
SCINDIA.

1892.

PREFACE.

THE FORT of GWALIOR being one of the most renowned and time-honored Fortresses in India, and possessing some rare specimens of Indian architecture, people come to see it from long distances. Since the connection of the Scindia State Railway with the Indian Midland Railway, the number of visitors is yearly increasing. The want of a true history of this noble structure, which has solemnly watched the rise, decline and fall of hundreds of Rajas, Maharajas, and Kings, and a true illustration of the old monuments raised at different times being frequently felt, I venture to publish this translation of a Small Persian Manuscript named "Gwalior Nama," up to General Popham's time, for the benefit of the Public.

B. S.

Lashkar, October 1891.

CONTENTS.

THE FORTRESS OF GWALIOR— PAGE

The Suraj Kund.............................. 3
Suraj-Pal, the Builder 5
Early History of the State 7
The Pal Dynasty ....9 and 11
Ram Deva Prahar.............................. 13
First Capture of the Fortress 15
A New Governor from Delhi 17
acquired by the Tanwar Rajputs.............................. 19
taken by Stratagem 21
in the hands of Raja Maun 23
The Goojri Mahal 25
captured by Humayun 27
visited by Mahomed Ghose 29
The Humayun Munzar 31
in Charge of Soor Bal 33
The Jahangeer Munzar.............................. 35
its Principal Buildings 37
besieged by the Mahrattas 39
surrendered to Rana Bhimsingh 41
in the hands of the Mahrattas.............................. 43
Defeat of the Deccanees 45
retaken by the English ....47—49
during the Mutiny 51
The Mutineers in Gwalior 53
restored to Maharaja Scindia..............................55, 56

THE FORTRESS OF GWALIOR.

THE Fortress of Gwalior stands on an eminence in the midst of an almost arid and stony plain. It stretches some two miles in length, and has a height of from 274 to 300 feet, with a breadth varying from 600 to 2,800 feet. Its origin, like that of the Cyclopean walls in ancient Greece, is shrouded in mystery. Later researches, made subsequent to the downfall of the Moghul dynasty and the advent of the British in India, connect the foundation of this stupendous structure in the third century after Christ (275 A.D.) with a memorable incident in the life of a Kutchwaha Thakur named Suraj Sen, who, from originally being the owner of a single village called Sehonia, lying at a distance of some 12 miles towards the east from the Fort, suddenly became the progenitor of a Royal race well-known in the annals of Gwalior.

Afflicted with leprosy for a period of two years, the Thakur happened, while on a hunting excursion, to pass by the site on which stands the now famous Fortress. Being faint with thirst and fatigue, and losing sight of the deer he had chased, the Thakur stopped short to find if he could any-how procure for himself a drink of water. There was nothing all around but dreary wilderness: solitary rocks standing in all the dismal solemnity of rugged loneliness, and wild flowers of spontaneous growth to be met with here and there, wasting their fragrance on the desert air. No human being was to be seen, nor any vestige of human habitation. Suddenly, to his agreeable surprise, the thirst-stricken Rajput espied a Jogee, or Hindu ascetic, standing at a little distance, who, in response to a request made to him, pointed out a spring under a tree hard by, and handing over to the applicant for water a piece of cloth or a large coarse handkerchief generally used by the Hindu Fakirs, desired him at the same time to fetch in it some of the contents of the spring for his, the hermit's, use. The injunction was strictly obeyed. Suraj Sen having performed his ablutions brought the liquid as safely and securely as if the coarse handkerchief was originally designed to hold the water of life. The ascetic, tasting the liquid and returning the piece of cloth to his uninvited guest, permitted him to quench his thirst to his heart's content, and then, looking wistfully into the Thakur's face, expressed his deep sympathy for the loathsome disease the latter was afflicted with. The only remedy he suggested at the time was to bathe in the very same spring on a Sunday morning, which fortunately happened to fall on the morrow of the memorable day when this unexpected interview took place. The Thakur having satisfied the demand of nature went back to his village, ruminating all the while in his own philosophic way on the occurrences of the day; and bringing his whole family and a train of dependents along with him, he dipped next morning into the spring as directed, and immediately found himself whole and clean. Having given large sums of money and numerous kine in charity to needy Brahmins, Suraj Sen, as much overjoyed at his speedy recovery as overwhelmed with gratitude, fell submissively at the feet of the ascetic in token of his inability to requite the service so unexpectedly and so disinterestedly rendered. The hermit, touched with the chivalrous simplicity of the Rajput, loaded him with blessings, suggested to him the propriety of having the bed of the spring widened and causing it to be built of pucca masonry if practicable, and finally advised him to lay the foundation of a Fortress in which shall reign a long line of kings of his own kith and kin, without let or hindrance, as long as they continued to take "Pal" for their patronymic. The Thakur, being the lord of the revenues of a single village, brought forward his slenderness of purse as an excuse for his inability to execute the commands laid on him in the form of advice, when the recluse, with a benign face so peculiar to Hindu hermits, delivered into the hands of the amazed Rajput a "Butwar," or a pouch, containing a few pieces of metal and flints, which he assured the recipient of this hidden treasure would prove more than equal to meet all the demands that might be made on his purse in the course of the construction of the buildings he had been directed to raise. Calling Suraj Sen then by the name of Suraj Pal, and placing the palm of his holy hand on the head of the newly created king, the hermit disappeared in an instant as if he never had had any existence at all.

The name of this "Jogee," who lived simply on the vegetables of the forest, was "Gwalpa Sidh," or the saint who received his illumination from his faith in the cowherds or playmates of the god Krishna, and the spring of water that restored Suraj Sen to his wonted health and strength, is now the well-known pucca-built Suraj Kund, or the spring dedicated to the Purifier and the Illuminator of the Universe.

Suraj Sen ascended the *guddee* under the name of Suraj Pal and brought the Rajas and Zamindars of the neighbourhood under his subjection. He had the satisfaction of seeing the noble Fortress brought to completion in his own lifetime. Several other buildings, like the pucca-built Suraj Kund, owed their existence to him. His rule was popular, and he led a very happy life indeed. Having reigned (36) thirty-six years with justice and moderation, and dying a natural death, he bequeathed his kingdom to his son Rasak Pal, who reigned only one year, and was succeeded by his own son, Narhar Pal, who raised a temple to the god Mahadeva which is still in existence. He also laid the foundation of a village called Narhar Tela, situated in the Kasba of Alapore. Being fond of hunting hogs, he lost his life in an attempt to slay a wild boar that eventually killed him. His reign lasted eleven years, ten of which were passed in unalloyed happiness. To him succeeded Amar Pal, father of Bhim-Pal, who caused a temple to be built, which is now known under the name of Bheemashwar. He reigned thirty-six years, and was succeeded by Gang Pal, who ruled twenty-one years, and built the celebrated Gangola lake. After him came Raj Pal, who reigned ten years and left the State to Bhoj Pal, during whose rule, of some nine years' duration, was erected the famous shrine of Chatar Bhooj Rai, or the god with four hands, one of the manifestations of the Hindu god Krishna. This edifice is unique in its character, being built of a single stone and situated near Bharonepore.

Padam Pal succeeded his father Bhoj Pal and reigned nine years. The shrine, dedicated to the god Latchmee Narayan, was raised under his auspices. His son and successor, Anang Pal, was reported to have met the celebrated "Gwalpa Sidh," who imparted to him the secret by which the alchemists of ancient times managed to convert the baser metals into gold. It was during his reign that gold Mohurs of five tolas in weight, manufactured at the Gwalior mint, were in circulation. He left the State to Indra Pal, who reigned only three years, and much oppressed the people. His successor, Jeet Pal, expired after a rule of fourteen years. The shrine of Jeetee Durga owes its origin to his artistic taste. After him Basant Pal ruled the kingdom for full seventeen years, and bequeathed it to Dhondo Pal, whose reign extended over eleven years. His successor, Latchman Pal, lived only four years after his coronation, and was succeeded by his son, Nahar Pal, who, during his brief reign of two years, laid the foundation of the village of Naharpore situated in the vicinity of the Fort. He was followed on the *guddee* by his son, Bhander Pal, who raised the Fort of Bhander and caused a tank to be sunk that still endures. He reigned eleven years, bequeathing the State to his son, Ajaz Pal, who governed it for nine years.

The history of some 20 successors to King Suraj Pal has now been recorded. It will be quite enough for the purpose in hand to give the bare names of the kings of the Pal dynasty who occupied the

Gwalior *guddee* subsequent to the reigns of those already mentioned :—

1. Aspal.
2. Sees Pal.
3. Bhoj Pal.
4. Bhairone Pal.
5. Gunpat Pal.
6. Chaura Sookh Pal.
7. Gaoo Munt Pal.
8. Nagish Pal.
9. Budh Pal.
10. Madh Pal.
11. Bir Pal.
12. Kant Pal.
13. Keerat Pal.
14. Danee Pal.
15. Bhip Pal.
16. Hamir Pal.
17. Chatar Pal.
18. Bhomindra Pal.

19. Dheer Pal.
20. Nagendra Pal.
21. Sudh Pal.
22. Sindhoo Pal.
23. Madhoo Pal.
24. Ovor Pal.
25. Budnu Pal.
26. Jay Pal.
27. Sandhan Pal.
28. Bal Bhadra Pal.
29. Gundharap Pal.
30. Saij Pal.
31. Devendra Pal.
32. Ramchandra Pal.
33. Dhondar Pal.
34. Saromand Pal.
35. Pardaman Pal.
36. Rasak Pal.
37. Deepak Pal.
38. Anant Pal.
39. Gaj Pal.

40. Jugddeesh Pal.
41. Gunjee Pal.
42. Ram-Deve Pal.
43. Seewani Pal.
44. Hirchand Pal.
45. Birakh Pal.
46. Tilak Pal.
47. Bijay Pal.
48. Dhander Pal.
49. Naig Pal.
50. Herlaik Pal.
51. Partab Rudra Pal.
52. Kaisar Pal.
53. Asad Pal.
54. Indera Pal.
55. Maun Pal.
56. Karam Pal.
57. Esar Pal.
58. Mon Pal.
59. Sagar Pal.
60. Bishambar Pal.

61. Ratan Pal.
62. Dhore Pal.
63. Budha Pal.

From Suraj Pal, the founder of the dynasty, to Budha Pal, the last on the above list, there had been eighty-four (84) kings, who reigned during a period of nine hundred and eighty-nine (989) years, under the patronymic of Pal—a solid proof of the long-continued peace enjoyed by India under her indigenous sovereigns. The son of Budha Pal rejoiced in the name of Tej-Karan, and the time had now arrived for the prophecy of the Saint "Gwalpa" "Sidh" to be literally fulfilled. Ran Mul, the Chief of Ambere (Jeypore), had a daughter, who, in course of time, was united in wedlock to Tej-Karan of Gwalior, who soon became much attached to a wife that brought with her very costly dowry in the shape of horses, elephants, and other valuable property. Being of a very prepossessing appearance, he was offered, while still a guest in the house of his father-in-law, succession to the sovereignty of Ambere, on condition of his consenting to make that capital his home, as the reigning sovereign of that place had no male issue of the body to succeed him in the event of his demise. The ambitious and calculating Tej-Karan at once closed with the offer: the State of Gwalior at that time being less in extent and value than the renowned kingdom of Ambere. During his absence from Gwalior, the affairs of the latter principality were managed by one Ram Deva Prahar, who, after two years of successful administration, formally applied to be recognized as the *de facto* ruler of the State. The application was granted, and the authority to rule and reign was thus duly transferred from the dynasty of Pal to the family of Prahars, of whom seven kings as noted below:—

1. Parmal Deva,
2. Salam Deva,
3. Bikram Deva,

4. Ratan Deva,
5. Sobhang Deva,
6. Narsing Deva,
7. Parmal Deva,

occupied the Gwalior *guddee* during a period of one hundred and two (102) years, after which the famous Fortress fell into the hands of the Sultan Shamsuddeen Altamash.

This Sultan was originally a slave of Kuttubuddeen Aibak, who, discovering in him the germ of a great mind, raised him to high offices in the State, and eventually made him his son-in-law by giving him his own daughter in marriage. On the death of Kuttubuddeen, his son-in-law ascended the throne of Delhi, and extended the limits of the Empire both in the south and on the eastern frontier. When returning from the conquest in the south, Altamash happened to encamp with 96,000 cavalry at the village of Antree, whence he beheld edifices of stupendous size and exquisite workmanship rearing their proud heads in the midst of a barren plain. It was soon brought to his notice that at a little distance from the encamping ground lay the renowned Fortress of Gwalior, where independent Rajas of the Kutchwaha branch of the ancient Solar race had reigned supreme for a long time without paying any tribute to the sovereigns of Islam. It also came to his knowledge at the same time that there was no Kutchwaha then in the fort to resist his advance, and that one Parmal Deva, of the family of Prahars, occupied the *guddee* in the place of the Kutchwahas with the latter's consent. The Sultan, binding himself with a solemn oath, ordered his nobles to seize the fort at once, and cause a mosque to be erected there forthwith. That very day the fortress was invested: while the besiegers and the besieged were busily employed in making requisite preparations to act respectively on the offensive and the defensive, the Emperor Shamsuddeen rode on horseback to take a view of the entire position, and, arriving at the place, which is now known as the

"Well of Jhilmil," he discovered there a weak point, with the eye of an experienced general, and managing to throw his men from that point into the Citadel, he came unawares on the Rajputs, who, having already immolated their female relatives on the funeral pyre, in accordance with the old usage of the heroic times, fought with desperate courage, but victory, in the end, declared itself for the followers of the Crescent. The Hindu king, who had become useless from the abuse of stimulants, and who would not suffer anybody to interfere with his pleasures, was now made acquainted with the real state of affairs. He soon fell a victim to the wrath of the invader, who put the whole garrison to the sword, and the family of the Prahars that had been reigning on sufferance thus came to an end.

It was in the afternoon that the battle was brought to a close, and by the evening a small mosque was erected, and the Mahomedan form of prayer recited to the great joy of the Sultan, who caused the

Khootba to be read in his name in accordance with the formal oath he had taken. Finding that there were only two tanks, the one, the well-known "Suraj Kund," and the other, the renowned "Gangola Lake" to supply the garrison with water, the Sultan ordered the adjacent lands belonging to the Fort to be enclosed within a wall on both sides, and within this enclosure he caused to be sunk numerous tanks and wells, many of which contained water so deliciously cool and pure that in the hottest weather no ice was required for cooling the drinks.

Meeran Yakoob, a nobleman of the Imperial Court, was now appointed Governor of the Citadel, and Bahadur Khan made a City Magistrate. Subsequently the Emperor left for Delhi, where he expired ten months after, and was succeeded on the throne by the Sultan Feroze and others, none of whom ever deputed a new Governor to the Fortress, which consequently continued in the hereditary charge of the Syads, appointed by the Sultan Altamash. In the reign of the Emperor Allauddeen, who added new countries to his Empire, there was a nobleman named Sikandar Khan who attended on the Sultan and had several persons in the service of the State under his command and control. Amongst these there were two Rajput brothers of the Tanwar clan of Rajputs named Parmal Deva and Adhar Deva, from the village of Esamamola, situated in the Perganna of Dandrolee. One night, while it was pitch dark and the rain falling in torrents, the Sultan happened to be standing at a balcony whence he beheld two soldiers standing on duty whilst the rest of their comrades were fast asleep. Both of them advanced towards the Emperor, who, on learning that they belonged to the Detachment under the command of Sikandar Khan, was much pleased with their conduct as evinced by their devotion to their duty. He permitted them to make any request, which would be at once granted. They related their story, which purported to be that they had always been true to their salt, but were unable to serve the State diligently so long as their children were wandering in the *jungle* for want of a decent home. They concluded their recital in the true Rajput fashion, with a request that Gwalior might be given to them as a place of residence for their families. The Sultan commanded them to be present at the Durbar the next day, when their petition would be granted without any further solicitation on their part. The sturdy Rajputs, well acquainted with the ways of Oriental Courts, represented the difficulties they were sure to encounter in attempting to have access to the Sultan in a formal Durbar. The Emperor, however, assured them of his good will towards them; and when, at the appointed hour, the two brothers stood at a respectful distance from the Audience Hall, the Sultan, proving as good as his word, summoned them both to his presence and gave them Gwalior as an Inam. They brought the mandate of the sovereign to the Syads in hereditary charge of the Fortress, but these pious gentlemen did not consider it worth their while to pay much attention to the *firman* that would have deprived them of their hereditary possession. The two Rajputs, however, continued their attendance on the Syads very submissively, and at last hit on a stratagem to achieve the desired end. As they had already ingratiated themselves by their submissive conduct into the favour of the Syads, the latter were asked to a dinner-party to be given in their honour at a village named Raneepura, whither the unsuspecting descendants of the grandsons of the Arabian Prophet repaired with their whole families. The food, mixed with intoxicating drugs, was served in the true Oriental style, and the guests, after partaking heartily of the meal that was to be their last on earth, retired to rest in the tents placed at their disposal by their hosts when, at a given signal, a band of Rajputs, who were concealed in a secluded place, rushed in with swords in their hands, and the poor sleeping innocents were murdered in cold blood for disobeying the mandate of their rightful sovereign. The sad news of the destruction of the Syads soon spread through the town, and a musician in their service who had been left in the Fort, on learning of the catastrophe, at once closed all entrances to the Citadel and began to beat the drum of war with his own hands at every gate of the stronghold where he knew the people passed by. This disconcerted for a time the plan of the Rajputs, who were led to suspect that there were still left in the Fortress people to mourn the loss of the Syads and avenge their death. The truth, however, becoming known on the third day, the musician prudently reconciled himself to the new state of things, when he was granted five villages in perpetuity for his maintenance. Thus came the family of the Tanwar Rajputs on the state in the drama of Gwalior politics and held the Fortress in their possession for a time. The names of the six kings of this family are given below, together with the periods of their respective reigns:—

Names of the Ruling Sovereign.	Duration of Reign.
1. Parmal Deva	6 years.
2. Zoodmorid Deva	5 „
3. Beeram Deva	15 „

Names of the Ruling Sovereign.	Duration of Reign.
4. Alan Deva	9 years.
5. Narsing Deva	25 ,,
6. Dongersing	30 ,,

Dongersing, the last of these six kings, built the gate of Ganesh Pole, situated near the third gate of Badalgurh. He also caused a well to be sunk, known under the name of Nagarwa, the virtues of the waters of which had passed into a proverb. It was so jealously guarded that no one was allowed to use its contents without previously obtaining the Royal permission. Diseases that baffled the skill and tried the patience of experienced physicians acknowledged the force of the healing powers of the nectar contained in the well of the Raja Dongersing, whose son, Kerat-singh, succeeded his father in due course, and built a lake of such gigantic dimensions that one extremity of it extended to the hillock of Bala Raja, and the other to the village of Shankarpore, the third side touching the heights known under the name of Adh

Badli, and the fourth stretching to the boundaries of the village of Akbarpore. This lake is now no more. In the midst of its ruins stands the mosque where the Mahomedans still recite their prayers twice a year on the well-known festivals of their two *Eeds;* and the sturdy husbandman of the period plies his plough where once existed the bed of the mighty lake designed and planned by a Raja of the Tanwar clan.

Keratsingh was succeeded by his son Kaliansingh, who reigned 27 years. His brother, named Badal, built the first gate of Badalgurh, which was called after his name. Raja Maun, the most famous of this clan, ascended the *guddee* on the death of his father Kaliansingh. He was a first-rate administrator and much feared and respected by his contemporaries. He subdued his enemies and took several forts. The celebrated Maun-Mandar with its gigantic gate owes its origin to his artistic genius. Each stone was worked upon for 26 days before it formed part of the building for which it was designed. The sculptor commenced his work on a certain propitious day, continuing his operations on the stone under the eye of a skilful master until the piece was brought to completion, on the day when the moon in her monthly course entered the most fortunate of her 27 mansions, well known to adepts in astrology. The edifices designed and planned by this Raja were, as a rule, picturesque and durable. Maun was fond of sporting excursions, and never denied himself the enjoyments and pleasures which this world afforded. The Brahmins and the Sahookars, to both of whom he was much attached, were very happy during his reign. In one of his sporting rambles in the neighbourhood of Rai, a village situated to the north-east of the Fort, he happened to meet a young damsel of extraordinary vigour and beauty, who once in an encounter with a wild-buffalo had subdued the latter with her bodily strength, as she now vanquished the brave Raja Maun with her fascinating eye. On enquiring from her the source of her strength, she said she owed all to her drinking copiously of the water of

Rai. In the hope of having strong healthy children the Raja offered to make her one of his wives, to which she consented, on condition of an arrangement being made for the water of Rai to reach the place of her residence in the Fortress. It was to this incident that the Gwalior people were indebted for the famous aqueduct, the traces of which are still to be seen in several places in the vicinity of the Fort. The renowned palace known as the Goojri-Mahal was the residence of this very damsel. The favourite queen of the Raja " Maun," however, was the Ranee-Mirg-Sal or the antelope-eyed queen, and the lake known as the Ranee Sagar, lying towards the southern extremity of the Fortress, was built in her honour and called after her name. A slave girl of this Ranee caused a tank to be constructed that had no water in it till an opening was made in the Ranee Sagar lake which poured its contents into the tank with the same profusion as the generosity of the lady-mistress had invariably relieved the wants of the slave girl.

The Fortress was in the possession of the Tanwar clan when Hoshang Shah, of Malwa, once laid siege to it in 1424. The contemporary of Raja Maun, however, on the throne of Delhi was Sultan Behlole Lodi who, having conquered Kalpi and the neighbouring countries, arrived at Dholpore *viâ* Chandawar, and the Chief of Dholpore had to purchase his freedom by offering several maunds of gold to the invader. The Sultan also received eighty lacs in money from the ruler of Gwalior, who, however, did not proceed in person to pay his homage to the Emperor, although invited to do so. Sikandar Lodi, the son of Behlole, on ascending the throne led his army to Kalpi, and leaving that country to the care of the princes of the blood, set his face towards Gwalior where the reigning Raja Maun had to offer him a larger amount of money than what was deemed sufficient to avert the wrath of his father the late Sultan. He moreover consented to have the Khootba read in the name of the Emperor, and also to acknowledge his suzerainty.

Bikramajeet, the last of the Tanwar race, succeeded Raja Maun, and reigned for three years. When the Sultan Ibrahim, the son of Sikandar Lodi, ascended the throne of Delhi, Azam Humayun, a nobleman of the Imperial Court, was sent to invest the Fortress of Gwalior in order to bring the ruling Raja to a sense of his duty. Piles of wood were placed before the gate of Badalgurh and set fire to. The invading force then entered the Citadel, and had to fight for every inch of ground, defended by the valour of the sturdy Rajputs. In the same manner three gates were taken possession of. At the fourth gate a noble Mahomedan fell while leading his men, and was buried there. The advancing column then returned towards the point whence it had started, and the Raja, finding himself unable to prolong the struggle, presented himself before the leader of the investing force, who sent him on to the presence of the Sultan who invested his subdued enemy with a dress of honour, and allotted the Pergana of Shamsabad for his maintenance. Azam Humayun was then appointed Governor of the Fortress, and the Hindu Sovereignty of Gwalior came to an end. From Parmal Deva to Bikramajeet there had been ten kings of the Tanwar race, who ruled during a period of 205 years.

The Emperor at Delhi began to entertain suspicions against the noblemen who had loyally served his father, and he felt no hesitation or compunction in destroying those that fell under his suspicion. Azam Humayun, who had a large following, could not be trusted with such a stronghold as that of Gwalior. He was accordingly executed, and his son, Salaimkhan, fearing the same fate awaited himself, went away towards the eastern frontier. Durbar Khan Lohanee, one of the most influential and trusted noblemen of the State, next fell a victim to the wrath of the suspicion-ridden Sultan. He was cruelly put to death, and the Lodees lost all confidence in their sovereign in consequence. They repaired first to the Punjab and thence proceeded to

Kabul, where they presented themselves before Baber, who treated them generously and held out expectations of redressing their grievances and rewarding their services in the near future.

Such was the state of affairs at the Imperial Court at Delhi when the renowned grandfather of the illustrious Akbar, and the friend and contemporary of the celebrated Sikh Guru Nanak, moved with a large army from Kabul. His march through the Punjab was almost a triumphal progress until he reached the plains of Paniput, where was fought a stubborn battle that ended in the total defeat of the forces of the Lodi Sultan, who was put to death, together with his friend the Raja Bikramajeet, once the ruler of Gwalior and now a Jagirdar of Shamsabad. The victorious Baber then marched on Delhi, and entering that ancient Capital in state deputed one Raheem Dadkhan to Gwalior to take charge of the Fortress there from Tartar Khan, a noble of the Lodi Durbar. Raheem Dadkan, however, soon fell under the displeasure of the Emperor like Khawaja Mehdi, the Subha of Lahore. He was thinking of taking refuge with Sultan Bahadur in Malwa, leaving the charge of the Fortress to the care of his trusted friend, the Rajput Parmokund, when there arrived at Gwalior the celebrated Mahomedan Saint, named Mahomed Ghose, who having brought the planet Mars under his sway by a peculiar form of devotion well-known to adepts in the science of mind, was thus enabled to influence the mind of kings, who honoured and respected him. Raheem Dadkhan waited on this saint, and through his intercession repaired to the Imperial Court where he was honorably received, his place at Gwalior having been at the same time filled by one Abdul Fateh, who was just in his dealings, and did all in his power to encourage trade by securing to the traders and the artizans the profits justly due to them.

Baber himself visited the Fort soon after and stayed there for a time. He laid a beautiful garden near the Gungola lake and caused an enclosure to be constructed in which congregated thousands of deer, and which thus served as a preserve for royalty. While living in the Fortress, the Emperor was afflicted with an ear-ache which was at last cured by the saint Mahomed Ghose breathing a prayer into the royal ear. Baber then left Gwalior for Agra and after a time was gathered to his fathers. His son, Humayun, who succeeded him, also paid a visit to the Gwalior Fort and built the edifice known under the name of Humayun Munzar. Sher Khan Sur subsequently raised the standard of revolt, and Humayun, after waging an unsuccessful war with his adversary, took refuge in Persia, whence he returned in time to regain his ancestral possessions.

Sher Khan, who ascended the throne after the flight of Humayun to Persia, stayed for a time at Gwalior, and the building known as Sher Munzar was raised under his orders. He lost his life by an explosion of gunpowder at the storming of the Fort of Kalinger, which he had laid siege to. His son, Jalal, ascended the throne under the name of Salaim Khan, and in the latter part of his life lived at Gwalior, where at last he gave up the ghost. The right of succession belonged to his son, Mobariz Khan, who, however, being a minor, was murdered by the husband of his father's sister, named Adil Khan, who then usurped the throne and gave himself up to worldly enjoyments. Enemies soon rose on all sides. Sikandar Khan and Ibrahim Khan, the sons of his own uncle, never acknowledged his authority. On the contrary, they took possession of all the districts they could lay their hands on. The Bania, named Heemoo, who in the commencement of his career had met with unusual success, was now the guiding genius of the administration. Things drew their slow length along in the manner stated above for a period of four years, when Adil Khan was killed in one of the battles brought on by his own unkingly conduct. During his reign the Fortress of Gwalior was in charge of a slave, named Soor Bal. After Adil's death the state of affairs in India was deplorable indeed. Every petty Chieftain became the Lord Paramount of the soil within his own territory, without acknowledging any controlling authority, and no stable government was in fact established until the return of Humayun from Persia. After the death of Humayun the illustrious Akbar ascended the throne, and India, that had become a desert for want of a controlling central authority, was now a smiling garden again under the fostering care of the new Emperor. The slave Soor Bal was still in charge of the Fortress at Gwalior. Ram Sahai, a son of the late Bikramajeet, gathering some Rajputs around him, attempted to take possession of the old stronghold, which he accordingly invested. Kaya Khan, a nobleman of the Court of Akbar, soon appeared on the scene with an army, and dislodging Ram Sahai from his position, brought his Artillery to bear on the Fort, which at last surrendered. For a period of 50 years during the reign of the Great Akbar the officials noted below held charge of the Fortress :—

1. Kaya Khan,
2. Alla Khan,
3. Syad Kasim,
4. Raja Askarn,
5. Raja Rajsing, son of Askaran.

During the reign of Akbar's son and successor, the well-known Jahangeer, the following Governors were in charge of the Citadel for a period of twenty-two years :—

1. Sheikh Bawa, brother of Mouzzam-Khan.
2. Nasir Oollah.
3. Ayar Khan.
4. Shujaat Khan (called Sheikh Kabeer).
5. Mahabat Khan.

6. Asaf Khan.
7. Har Narain.
8. Tatar Khan.

Mahabat Khan during his governorship submitted to the Emperor a document in which it was shown that the buildings known as the Humayun Munzar and the Sher Munzar, stood contiguous to each other, and that the former, built by his grandfather, was of an inferior description to the latter, which had been raised by his rival, the notorious Sher Khan. Jahangeer ordered the demolition of the Sher Munzar, the materials of which were utilized in building the edifice known as Jahangeer Munzar. This noble building was erected during the governorship of Raja Har Narain, who was a right virtuous man, and held the ascetic and the recluse in great estimation. He was a friend to all, without distinction of caste and creed, and took every opportunity of helping those he came in contact with. His successor, Tartar Khan, was given to prayers and devotions, and fond of associating with the learned and the devout.

Shah Jahan ascended the throne on the death of his father, Jahangeer, and it was during his reign that the governorship of the Fortress was conferred on the Barah Syads, a people well-known in the Mahomedan annals for their valour and munificence. The head of the party was Syad Meran Muzaffar. The following are the names of the governors who held charge of the Fortress under the Emperor Shah Jahan :—

1. Syad Muzaffar.
2. Syad Alam.
3. Meeran Syad.
4. Mahabat Khan.

Alamgir succeeded Shah Jahan and appointed Kwaja Abdulla Khan to the governorship of the Gwalior Fortress; a severe famine was raging at the time. Khwaja Abdulla signalized his tenure of office by making an arrangement by which all travellers, whether Hindus or Mahomedans, whe ther in actual want or not, who put at the two Serais or inns in the town, were to be fed at the expense of the State. He held his post for two years and was succeeded by Motmid Khan, who continued to discharge his duties at Gwalior for a period of seven years, during which he raised the following buildings:—

1. Alamgeer Gate.
2. Great Mosque with Hamam and Gate (bathing room).
3. Noorabad village and a Serai in it.

Motmid Khan was relieved by Khidmatgar Khan, who was a well-meaning man and beyond all praise. During his six years' tenure of office the following buildings came into existence:—

1. Dhorapore Baradaree.
2. Mola Fasil Garden.
3. Oorwai Gate.

When recalled to Delhi, he took along with him the three Princes—

1. Sultan Mahomed,
2. Dara Shikoh,
3. Morad Bux,

who were confined in the Fort. Syad Munaovar Khan was then sent to Gwalior to discharge the duties of Governor there. He was as brave as he was kind and charitable. The men who had suffered from the rash proceedings of Mahomed Ali, steward to the late Khidmatgar Khan, were restored to their former emoluments with certain additions on his part. He endeared himself to the people, with whom he much sympathized, and made over charge of his duties to his successor, the Nawab Shayasta Khan, when commanded by his sovereign to do so. The Nawab was, however, recalled and his place taken by Basant Shah, who held the post until his death, which took place during the reign of Mahomed

Shah. He lies buried in the naked Fakir's garden on the bank of a river by the side of the public road that leads to the Kasba of Antree. His brother, Kasid Ali Khan, was appointed in his place and deserved well of the people. His tomb is situated near Gohad, on the public road leading to Gwalior.

The descendants of the Great Tamerlane were generally endowed with all the qualifications of successful administrators, but no Dynasty can claim to continue its reign for ever and ever in this world of change and revolutions. During the reign of Mahomed Shah the administrative machinery was out of gear. The king was devoted to sensual enjoyments, and never looked into the affairs of the State—troubles rose on all sides. The people in the Deccan asserted their independence. The governors charged with the care of provinces sought safety in flight, and Mahratta armies overran the whole country. In the reign of Alamgeer the Second, a Mahratta force encamped outside the walls of Delhi, whence rich bankers and honourable gentlemen began to fly. Vithal-Rao Bahadur, a Sirdar in the Deccan Army, had been for several years in the District of Gwalior, and easily managed to bring under his subjection the neighbouring zamindars, who cheerfully paid the Government dues to him. In a word, all matters relating to the police and the revenue administration were referred to him for decision, and he left no stone unturned to promote the interests of those who had deputed him. Finding the circumstances favourable, he attempted to take possession of the Gwalior Fortress, when the Rajputs in the service of the King of Delhi continued a desultory fight for a month, during which the people in the town suffered much, as batteries were erected by the invaders before the Mosque situated in the midst of the city. The men within the fortress, who never thought of fighting seriously, were as secure from wounds and injuries as a lady in her *zenana*. At last, in consultation with Kishan Das, the "Modi" to the Killadar, it was decided that the Citadel should be surrendered to the Rana Bhimsingh of Gohad, in preference to the people of the Deccan. Accordingly some three hundred men of the Rana were allowed to enter the Fortress by the way of the "Kabootar Khana." They were soon followed by the Rana himself, who, accompanied with soldiers, both on foot and horseback, took up a position at the village of Goorganwan. The Rao Vithal of Deccan was now forced to raise the siege, and the Rana entering the Citadel expelled all the idlers who had no experience of actual warfare. The Rajputs in the service of the King of Delhi were also turned out, as they had behaved no better than their friends and companions mentioned above. The Mahomedan Killadar was, however, permitted to retain his post, he being a man of position and having access to the Emperor. The people of Gwalior were well cared for during the Rana's *regime*. At last, after two months and-a-half the force of the Rao Vithal of Deccan surrounded the village of Bahadurpore. Resultless skirmishes took place every day without doing much harm to either side. One day, as the Rana came out of the Fort and took his stand at the village of Saloo, merely to take a view of the position, and not to give battle, the forces on both sides took the initiative without any word of command from their respective leaders. The Rana being in the midst of the field of battle performed prodigies of valour, and receiving a mortal wound retired to the Citadel, where he expired three days after, and was burned near the great tank in accordance with Hindu usage. A Mahomedan dancing girl, named Roushan, a favourite of the Rana, ascended the funeral pyre of her late master with all the calmness of a devoted Hindu wife. The troops of Vithal Rao then entered the town with all the appliances of war in their possession, and Kanwar Mulju, the son of the late Rana, took the place of his father in the Fort. For several months a desultory fight continued, until a compromise was effected by which a "Thana" of the Deccan people was established within the walls of the stronghold with the consent of both parties.

Vithal Rao was as brave as he was generous, and the people of Gwalior District expected nothing but good at his hands. Having endeared himself to all he came in contact with, the Rao returned to give an account of his stewardship at Gwalior to his superiors in the Deccan, where he soon expired. His son, Bapu Shivaji Vithal, was then deputed to take the place of his noble Sire at Gwalior. He trod in the footsteps of his father and was soon a favourite with his followers. A subordinate official under him, named Gobind Shamrao, looked after the State business for a period of twenty-six years with great credit, and died at Gwalior to the regret of all. He was burned in accordance with Hindu usage at a spot where subsequently was raised a temple to the god Mahadeva as a tribute to his memory, and where in his own life-time he had laid two gardens and had caused two tanks to be sunk. The garden, called the Nazar Bagh, situated in the vicinity of the Ladhairee hills, also owed its existence to his love of gardening. To him was due the merit of raising a substantial building on the site where the celebrated "Gwalpa Sidh," the patron and the benefactor of the Pal Dynasty, once performed his devotions. Gobind Shamrao had once held the post of a Subha in the Deccan, and his son, Raghunathrao, was now sent to Gwalior to take the place of his father.

The Raja Chatarput of Gohad, a son of Kanwar Mulju, mentioned above, had kept up the struggle with the Deccanees. He was a young man of great promise and known for his martial exploits, not only in Hindustan and the Deccan, but also in countries inhabited by Europeans. His influence was so great that the zamindars of their own accord acknowledged him as their lord and master. The protracted struggle between him and the Deccanees, however, reduced the people of Gwalior to such straits that many of them left the town and took up their abode in villages at a distance from the seat of disturbance and war. For several years affairs continued in this state. At last Bapuji Holkar, a Sirdar from the

Deccan, appeared with a large force, and a decisive battle took place that ended in the total discomfiture of the Deccanees, whose Artillery and camp fell into the hands of their victorious antagonists.

The Deccanees, although defeated, were not subdued. Another army with a large number of guns advanced from the Deccan under the command of Bhau Saheb and Vishwas Rao. Their number was estimated at one lakh of sowars at the least. They spread themselves like locusts from the wilds of the Deccan to the banks of the Attock. No Raja in India found himself capable of opposing their advance. When they stopped at Gwalior on their way to Northern India, and took a view of the adjacent country from the heights of the Gwalior Fortress, they expressed their regret at their inability to punish the Gwalior malcontents for want of time. They, however, declared their firm resolve to carry their threats into execution on their victorious return from the North. Proceeding onwards with a firm belief in their own invincibility, they gave battle to Shah Abdali, who, however, routed them with great slaughter. Bhau Saheb, the leader of the Deccan army, fell in the midst of the field of battle, and such of his followers as escaped the vengeance of the conqueror's sword sought safety in flight.

From the Sammat year 1836 to 1837, the Deccan army, led by Ambajee Inglea and Gunpat Rao, a son of Bapuji and grandson of the late Vithal Rao, continued to engage with the force under the command of the Raja Chatarput of Gohad. The Sirdar Khanderao also accompanied the Deccan army and held a position in no way inferior to his brethren in arms. When hard pressed by his enemies the Rana of Gohad applied for, and obtained the aid of the English, whose presence alone sufficed to produce a depressing effect on the Deccanees, who in parties of from ten to twelve men began to make themselves scarce when pitted against the disciplined British force. For several months the situation remained unchanged. The leaders of the Deccan army then began to separate themselves from their men, and the rumour got abroad that a kind of truce had been effected. Ambajee Inglea with a small force entered Gwalior and the British troops took up a position at the village of Raipore, some eight miles from the city. Two companies of the Deccan army garrisoned the Fortress, but took no precautionary measures against a surprise. On Friday, the 4th of the Hindu month of Shrawan, when the sun, according to the Hindu mode of calculation entered a new constellation, two Regiments under the command of British officers scaled the heights of the Fortress with the help of ladders early in the morning by the way of Gargaj. No opposition was offered to their advance, Bapuji Subadar and other Deccan Sirdars did certainly come out and advanced as far as Suraj Kund with the express intention of offering resistance to the invading British force, but not being adequately supported by their followers, they retraced their steps, when the Subadar Bapuji fell dead from a musket shot. Two sepoys carried his corpse to the Kotwali, where it was burnt after the Hindu fashion. Ambajee Inglea, taking as much property as he could possibly carry along with him, marched off by way of Pahargurh, together with the force under his command. The English were now masters of the Fortress, and they lost no time in proclaiming to the public by beat of drum that no one was to be molested in the pursuit of his peaceful avocation, as long as he continued loyal and faithful to the State that protected him. The name of the leader of the British force and the conqueror of the Fortress was General Popham, his title being Asad-ud-doula Ameen-ul-mulk which, translated into English, would be the "Lion of fortune" and "The trusted Noble of the Realm."

The above is generally a free translation of a Persian Manuscript called "Gwalior Nama" which was originally prepared from materials furnished by a learned Brahmin whose family enjoyed the privilege of officiating at worship in the Fort both under the Hindoo and the Mahomedan Sovereignties.

Since General Popham's time, the Gwalior Fortress has witnessed other vicissitudes of fortune to which everything mundane is liable as a matter of course. The victorious British General had made over the Citadel to the Rana of Gohad, but Mahadji Maharaj, the illustrious founder of the Scindia Dynasty, retook it in A.D. 1782, as much by his consummate generalship as by his skill in diplomacy. It was then placed in charge of Ambajee Inglea who was appointed as a Soobah of the Scindias for the District of Gwalior. Infected with the contagion of the times, the Soobah undertook to surrender the Fortress in 1803 to the officers of the East India Company; but at the same time secretly instructed the Commandant not to deliver it up at the appointed hour. This led to the investment of the stronghold by the British troops, who took it by assualt on the 5th of February 1804. After the

7

cessation of hostilities, when a treaty of peace had to be concluded between the Scindia Durbar and the Government of the Company, the question arose as to the disposal of the Gwalior Fortress. Sir John Malcolm, the acknowledged father of the most illustrious School of British Indian Diplomacy, was for restoring the Citadel to the Scindia family for several weighty reasons, but the Marquis of Wellesley, the then Governor-General who, forced by the exigencies of the times, had to employ different Agents in different parts of India to negotiate treaties of peace with the Native Princes, had already promised the cession of the stronghold to the Rana of Gohad, who accordingly got possession of it. This proved very distasteful to the Maharaja Doulatrao Scindia, who had succeeded Mahadji Scindia on the latter's demise. Circumstances, however, soon changed, and Sir John Malcolm had the satisfaction of concluding a treaty with the Gwalior Durbar by which the noble Fortress was restored to the possession of the Scindias as much in the interests of justice as of policy.

Since then the famous stronghold continued in the undisturbed possession of the Scindia family until the year 1857, when there occurred a military revolt in India, the Native Contingent stationed at Morar and commanded by British officers, following the example of their brethren, in other parts of the country, broke into open mutiny. The European officers and their families, together with the British Resident, Major Macpherson, had made their way to the Maharaja's Palace, at Lushkar, whence they were safely escorted to Agra. The youthful Maharaja, Jiajee Rao, the ruler of Gwalior, was then in the 24th year of his age and altogether without any experience. The force of his personal character and the prestige of the family to which he belonged, however, stood him in good stead, and he succeeded as well in saving the life of his Minister, Sir Dinkar Rao, from the wrath of an infuriated soldiery as in restraining hosts of insurgents from proceeding to Delhi, where their presence would have augmented the fighting powers of the rebels to a most dangerous extent. So vast was the number of the insurgents congregated at Gwalior with all the appliances of war in their possession, that, when failing to induce the young Maharaja to head the rebellion, they were most adroitly prevailed upon to leave his Capital in any directon save that of Delhi ; they set out towards Cawnpore where they soon succeeded in reducing General Wyndham to sore straits, but were in their turn literally annihilated by Sir Colin Campbell, the British Commander-in-Chief, who, relieving the beleaguered garrison at Lucknow and escorting the ladies and children of the garrison to Calcutta, had by a happy coincidence arrived at Cawnpore just in time to extricate his friend, the hero of the Redan, from the awkward and miserable plight the latter was in.

In the meanwhile Sir Hugh Rose, leading his small but compact force from victory to victory throughout the whole of the Central India campaign, had relinquished its command after the conquest of Kalpi, where the work cut out for him was brought to a close.

The fugitive rebels from Kalpi with the intrepid Ranee of Jhansi and the Nawab of Banda in their midst, managed somehow to arrive, though in a state of utter destitution, at Gwalior, where every arrangement for their friendly reception had been secretly made by the archschemer, the notorious Tantia Topay, whose subtle and dexterous proceedings during the military revolt are well known to the readers of the Mutiny literature. The youthful Maharaja saw at once that Tantia Topay was the master of the situation and he had to bow to necessity. Beset by the rebels and deserted by his disciplined troops, the proud Mahratta Prince had to leave his Capital, though much against his will for Agra, where he was cordially received by the British authorities in the Fort. In whatever light this might be regarded, there can, however, be no denying of the important fact that the ruler of Gwalior with all the prestige of his illustrious family symbolised in his person, by thus publicly declaring himself on the side of the British Government, contributed not a little to break the neck of the rebellion that was still at its height. In his absence the insurgents ruled supreme in his Capital for full 17 days, during which they plundered the Treasury and indulged in licenses of all sorts.

Sir Hugh Rose, on learning the state of affairs, rejoined the force destined to relieve Gwalior and restore the Maharaja Scindia to his ancestral possessions. The Mahratta Prince started at the same time from Agra, and joining the camp of the Agent to the Governor-General, arrived at the Cantonment, at Morar, which was at once wrested from the hands of the insurgents. Fighting continued for three days, during which the valiant Ranee of Jhansi, the only warrior of note among the rebels, fell dead by the spear of a British Hussar, and was immediately burnt on the spot by her adherents. The Fort of Gwalior was still held by a handful of the mutineers who were determined to sell their lives dearly, but it was soon taken by an assault, in which a nephew of the gallant General Sir Hugh Rose had to give his life in the service of his country. The Maharaja was replaced on the "Guddee" of his ancestors amid the rejoicings of his people, and his State was restored to him whole and entire. But the occupation of the Fort by a British garrison for a time was deemed expedient in the interests of the Maharaja, whose right to its possession was demonstrated by the flying of His Highness' flag from the ramparts of the Citadel. The Fortress was finally restored to the Maharaja Jiajee Rao in 1886.

The noble stronghold is now in the undisputed possession of the Scindia Dynasty, and that it may continue to remain for ever and ever in their possession, is the fervent prayer and the heartfelt wish of the present writer, who has the honor to belong to the same illustrious family.